Shadow Gods and Black Fire

Andrew Gyll

Illustrated by Abby Helasdottir

Shadow Gods
and
Black Fire

Andrew Gyll

Illustrated by Abby Helasdottir

Hubbardston, Massachusetts

Asphodel Press
12 Simond Hill Road
Hubbardston, MA 01452

Shadow Gods and Black Fire
© 2008 Andrew Gyll
ISBN 978-0-578-00653-6

Cover Art © 2008 Abby Helasdottir
Cover model: Jhana Millers

Printed in cooperation with
Lulu Enterprises, Inc.
860 Aviation Parkway, Suite 300
Morrisville, NC 27560

To Lizard Woman, my family,
the Fireflies and other friends
who have encouraged
and put up with me!

Contents

Foreword

Her mystery is a scent
of rot upon the air,
a curl of smoke
from the funeral pyre;
she is red meat
in the raven's beak,
the earth's open mouth
gaping
in mute anticipation.

Until the day that the Goddess walked out of the waves at Hengistbury Head (see poem of that name) I had worked almost exclusively with the Deities of the Roman and Greek pantheons. From that day, however everything changed for me. These poems speak of life, death and regeneration. There is darkness, but I hope also some light. As Hodur explains in 'Baldur', light and dark both require the presence of the other in order to be truly seen and appreciated.

This book comprises a series of dreams, visions and insights received over a period of about three years. It concerns primarily the mysteries of creation and regeneration, both of worlds and the individual.

The first section, 'Shadow Gods and Black Fire' is my personal exploration of the Norse mythology and religion in general and the Rökkr, the strange shadow Gods of that tradition, in particular. The second part, 'The Dís' is concerned with ancestral wisdom, being a series of reminiscences recounting the life and experiences of a particular female ancestor, or Dís.

As this is a book of poetry, I have fought down the temptation to write long and no doubt tedious essays detailing the mythological and personal background to the poems. I have, however, added some brief notes and suggestions for further reading at the back of the book.

Notes on Pronunciation

First a brief word about pronunciation. The names used in this work are mostly Norse, and as such shouldn't prove too difficult for English speakers. Put very simply:

Rökkr rhymes with **worker**.

Dís rhymes with **peace**.

Aur at the beginning of names like **Aur**gelmir and **Aur**vandil sounds more or less like English **hour**.

G is always hard as in **g**et.

J is pronounced like an English **y**.

Y (rather more awkward!) is like a German **ü**. The closest English equivalent would be the **oo** sound in s**oo**n and m**oo**n.

Part 1:

Shadow Gods and Black Fire

: ᛁᚾᚪᚠᛖ·ᛒᛁ ᛈᛏ ·ᚠ·ᛒᚪᚪᛏ:

:ᚩᚠ·ᛚᚪᚳᚳᛖᚱ·ᚹᚪᚱᚺᛋ:

:ᚺᛖᚱ·ᛋᛁᛏ·ᚩᚠ·ᛋᛁᚠᚹᛖᚱ:

: ᛁ ᚾᚪᚠᛖ·ᛋᚳᚾᛏ:

:ᚠᛁᚾ·ᛁ ᚾᚪᚠᛖ·ᚱᛋᚺᛗᛘ:

:ᚺᛖᚱ·ᛈᚪᛋᛏ·ᚩᚠ·ᚷᛖᚺᛘ:

:ᛏᚪᚱᚾᛁ·ᛒᛖᚠᚪᚱᛖ:

:ᚦᛖ·ᛋᚾᛏ:

Skald

There is a wood
where birches shimmer,
glowing ghosts
beneath a piebald sky.

In the wood
there is a pool
fringed with reeds,
surface lightly creased
by the passage of birds.

Out on the water
a song comes swimming,
sweet as a spinning ring,
white as snow
or the chalky hill's breast.

I must learn it,
hunt it ... dip
my silken arrow's tip
into the swan's red heart.

A silver thread,
I must spin it;
a silver song,
I must sing it;
a silver message
I must send it
far beyond
the dappled moon.

Magpie Woman

Always, she comes
in the smoking shadows
of autumn's end,
in the leaves
mounded up
and mouldering
at the forest's fringe.

In all things she is liminal,
dwelling at colour's boundary,
within the edge of being,
on the perfect point
of Skadhi's arrow,
where the hiss and thud
of life and death
spiral together,
spiral apart.

She is transition;
one black wing,
one white,
warm flesh,
cold bone.

Queen and corpse,
she is grace and horror
residing in the dark.

She is life
that has withered,
the promise of beauty
yet to come.

Hengistbury Head

It is Modron and it is dark.

The wind whips in
and the waves
are grey streamers,
dimly seen,
rushing for the shore.

It becomes darker
when the blindfold tightens;
cut off from everything
I could weep with relief.

How does the blind man
know when someone approaches?

Soft hands take mine
and guide me down
across the stones;
within the veil I can see
turquoise clouds churning,
racing overhead.

The Goddess comes
out of the sea,
dripping with snakes.

She divides,
becomes two,
becomes three,
begins to sway,
to circle.

Despite the dance
she is not kind,
her words are not gentle;
she berates,
demanding the snake
offer up his pain,
surrender his desperation.

She coalesces,
becomes two,
becomes one.

She demands the snake
give up his skin.

The Call

Neither tender nor cruel
her words are mineral;
water and stone,
a mist to still
the muffled land,
new snow lying
thick with time
and memory
upon the hills.

I am dead.

But this death is not harsh.
I lie sprawled, passive,
blue-faced and bloated,
unseeing eyes tipped upwards,
lifeless as clouded glass.

There is no sensation
beyond the hardness of bone,
the softness of tissue,
the relief of dissolution.

I am devoured.

Downwards
into the earth I sink.

I am an odour
of putrefaction,
a taste of rot
in the soil—and then,

I am ... nothing.

There is, however, no end.

Adjusted,
amended,
reassembled,
I rise as vapour
to stand before her.

Her eyes are blue fire,
white face, black hair,
black face, white hair,
her robe is razor blades
and shattered mirrors.

She speaks.

Now, do you see?

I am Hela.
I have called you,
you will serve me
and I will be there
when your time comes.

It is cold and clear.

It is glacial.

I am in love.

Mordgud

The bridge is slick
beneath his feet;
a million razors,
edges upmost.

He is not, however, afraid
and this surprises him
though he knows
that this lack of fear
is exactly why
the blades do not cut him.

Having crossed,
he kneels on the chill earth,
head bowed,
his breath, steam,
sobbing forth
on the sharp air.

She stands before him,
yellow hair
and eyes blazing
like green fires;
lips, the pink
of roses, pursed.

Why are you here?
You're not dead yet.

He cannot speak,
the words stick in his throat;
she continues.

You may pass, I don't mind,
but why do you want to?

He breathes and stammers—
I don't know what to do!

She pauses and nods.

Why don't you go away
and think about it?

Truth

His eyes cold fire,
Our Lord of Mayhem
whispers in my ear.

Lie to whomsoever you will
but not to yourself!

What are you afraid of?
Faceless authority
that bends you to its will,
commands and tames you?

Is that your fear ... or
is it your desire?
And what other secrets
do you keep?

Even in your poems
you never tell them
how you kneel and mourn
beside the graves
of all those other lives.

You never say
how lonely it is
to toil beneath
those years
that only **you** think wasted.

You never admit
how you long
to huddle in the hollow

of my daughter's
dark wing;
how hard it is
when she says—
you have mind and wings
of your own,
now fly, my chick!

He rocks back
on his heels,
his three cornered smirk
a question to which
I have no answer.
Still, Lord, enough!

More gently now,
he offers his hand.

Enough, indeed,
this life *is* enough!

He lifts his face
and laughs at the moon.

See, Mani is come
to pipe us home!

And so ... arm
in improbable arm,
in improbable silence,
we walk the white paths
through the heather,
the Moon God dancing
madly before us.

Surt

I was first.

I am the doorkeeper
who will drop the bolts
behind you when you leave.

In the leap, twist,
and salamander slither
I writhe and seethe
in formlessness.

I am breath
and the mother of smoke.

I am warmth and terror,
the dance at the star's heart.

I am fury
on the face of the atom.
I am molten.

I am love, death,
terror and exaltation.
I am the beginning of beginnings
and the end of ends.

I am the doorkeeper
who will drop the bolts
behind you when you leave.

Grandmother says she is oldest—
I am older.

One-eye says he is wisest—
I am wiser.

Red-beard says he is strongest—
I am stronger.

World-walker says he is the most cunning—
I am slyer.

More terrible than Hel,
with her I gather parings
at the end of time.

My sons have honed
their swords of flame;
in splendour they spring forth
to ravage worlds
without number.

I am the doorkeeper
who will drop the bolts
behind you when you leave.

Ask and Embla

Imagine the grating
of fingernails on bark.

A penetration of wit and magic,
sharper than any knife,
a shaping more brutal
than that of any axe.

Imagine the gifts:
life, sense, and fire;
the gradual birth of sight
and half-formed understanding.

And then...
imagine departure.

They say 'shore'
and one thinks of sand and sunlight;
it was not like that.

A chill sea,
choked with fog,
surged in the Gap,
swollen by roaring streams
born of ice.

We huddled
in the lee of a boulder,
shivering,
and watched them go,
lost in themselves;
three forms, indistinct,

fading into the vague distance.

To them it was no big thing,
this deed of creation,
an act of impulse,
no more.

The Three Brothers

The spear, the fire
and the cup,
all different,
conjoined ... they make a whole.

This is their mystery.

From my vantage point,
an age away,
I saw the young Gods
emerge from the mist;
faces set, purpose fixed,
they loped like wolves
across the frozen land.

Aurgelmir was sleeping
—nothing unusual there—
and as they approached
he stirred, snorted,
and then, slept on.

Hauling themselves up
onto the giant's shoulder
two of the brothers
began to slash and hack
at his neck.

In no time they were covered with gore,
but their efforts
only served to waken him.

He tried to roar

and stagger to his feet,
but the third god,
having listened carefully,
plunged his whip-sharp sword
into the Old Man's chest
and pierced his heart.

A single drop
of crimson blood
leapt up to speck his cheek,
to mar his impassivity.

Ve speaks.

(His hair is the colour of blood and fire,
his heavily freckled face bronze.
All that he wears is scarlet;
in fact everything about him is red,
everything except his eyes which sparkle
like emerald fires.)

In a way,
I mourn the Old Man,
but it was no life.

He slept and ate,
farted and snored—
a belch was
as good as it got.

They won't have it,
but in murder
we made him new;
there must be movement,

change,
creation as a vortex
not a stagnant pool.

In death, Aurgelmir
gave rise to worlds,
to a Universe
of possibilities.

Yes, I mourn him,
but I am not much given
to regret.

Odin speaks.

(His hair, once gold,
is now the colour of iron,
his single remaining eye
is blue and piercing—
the empty socket is covered
with a plain patch
of black leather.)

It was never
in my nature
to slip through time,
an unmarked figment
of Ymir's torpid dreaming.

Mine, rather,
to shape worlds ,
to father and foster
Gods and men.

To hold in my hands
life and death,
glory, honour,
torment and triumph.

Even Gods
grow older and wiser;
now I wander
and scheme
as, then, I soared
and struck
like an eagle.

Vili speaks.

(He is pale,
hair almost white,
eyes grey but not cold;
he is clearly a thinker.)

I have little to say.

Usually so different,
my brothers appeared alike
as they chopped
at the Old Man.

There was blood everywhere.
I thought a moment,
found the soft spot,
plunged in my sword
to still his rumbling heart.

That is all.

All-Father

Wisdom and knowledge
are the winds on which
he rides.

One thing, above all,
he has learned;
no god is all-wise.

He has cast me down,
extracted oaths.

He has lifted me up
and enlightened me.

He has released me
and set me on my path.

His single eye is a blue star
blazing in space.
I do not understand him.
His purposes are
inscrutable as mist;
he knows the worlds
must move on,
yet ever seeks
to avert the cataclysm,
the day of doom
and his own
inevitable twilight.

Frigga

She is the beauty
of heaven and earth,
a birch grove
beneath the blue sky.

Her voice is measured,
quiet but firm.

She speaks.

Then it was different;
there was stagnation,
tedious aeons
stretched out before us;
Ymir's people were
half asleep, moribund,
while Bor, the first maker,
was half awake.

This way and that he went
building, shaping, doing;
the giants thought he was mad
but he carried on,
was never still.

His sons were like him
but their aim was higher;
they desired the making of worlds
and in the Old Man they found
untamed matter to work with.

Now it is different.

Ve and the giants seek change,
movement, the chaos
that brings new life
and vitality;
Odin and the Gods defend order,
our place at the tree's head,
those things good and fine,
we believe—in our pride—
should last for ever.

Vili is silent;
he watches the deep currents.

His people keep the balance.

The Old Queen And The New

In Jormungrund
the only sounds
are weeping rain
and the wind moaning
across the fells.

Almost unnoticed,
the old Queen is gone.

Her throne sits empty,
the iron gates are closed,
the dead are banished
to nest in trees,
to huddle in hollows
and shadowed pools,
to wander the worlds
and bathe in the meanders
of muddy streams.

Impossibly quiet,
yet not quite silent
they chitter in the damp,
dark corners of awareness.

They haunt creation.

Almost unnoticed,
the old queen is gone,
but the sound of her absence
grows louder.

*

I saw the child labour
across the snowfield,
limping, head bowed
into the relentless wind.

She muttered and
I thought her mad
till I saw the shifting forms
of death about her.

Hela! Hela! Hela!
they called.

Through ice-scarred lips
her reply grated.

Show me the way to the Iron Gates!

Ahead they leapt
through gust and flurry.

Queen! Queen! Queen!

Long the road is
and hard, so hard,
across nine chill days,
down nine dark nights.

Will you come,
will you open the Gates again?

I will come!

Every broken step
will I tread,
every pain endure.

For me, and me alone
the Gates will open.

The Iron Wood

The wood, itself,
is close and dark.

Trees lean and stoop,
bending down
as if to hear
each whisper,
to see each nuance.

Even the passage
of the smallest creature
is remarked.

The forest is alive,
an amalgam of wood and moss,
damp stone and awareness.

There is no place like it,
the very air is thick
with enchantment.

Nothing is as it seems.

Each breath, each step
is an act of magic;
effects ravel out
through all the worlds
in waves and eddies
sensed but not perceived.

Angrboda

Nowhere, save
in the Iron Wood,
were the exiled dead
made welcome.

Skulls of men and beasts
were fixed to poles
and twisted trunks,
offerings made
to the rocks
on which they rested,
to the dark pools
in which they bathed.

The Lady of that place,
the Mother of Wolves,
paid heed to their whispers.

Even the source
must have its centre,
a single point
from which
enchantment throbs.

In a tangled grove,
a ring of tumbled stone,
there the Oak-witch
and her flame-haired lover lay.

There they made Gods
to rival those above,
smoke and shadow

to balance their light.

Three times she burned,
three times to rise again
as blood and charcoal,
a taste upon
her husband's cunning tongue.

Dry ash revived
by steaming life she rose,
a question on her lips.

Where are my children?

Dry ash revived
by steaming life she rose,
red hatred in her heart.

They say she is
the Mother of Monsters,
the Bringer of Anguish.

She does not care
what they call her;
she is beyond all that.

She is the dark womb
in which we die,
and then are born again.

Loki

Loki! Lord!
World-walker!
Flame-hair!

You are the salmon
in the sunlight
leaping the weir,
the sharp eyed falcon
hunting on high.

You are the fierce dance
of the lightning,
the wildfire that devours.

You are inspiration,
penetration;
your embrace is heat,
your kiss embers
upon my lips.

Storm-child!
Fire-hawk!
Bright-eyed Schemer!

They say you are faithless,
but I have faith!

They say you are sly.
I say you are clever!

They say you are chained,
I say you are free!

You are natural!

Loki! Lord!
You carry a piece
of my smoking heart;
may I be born again
through you!

World Serpent

Sleek, despite her immensity,
her motion is the tumult
that drives the sea.

She is wild time;
all our futures,
all our pasts,
encapsulated
in the crushing pressure
and smoking blackness
of the ocean floor.

She is turbulence and chaos
and, yet, the girdle
that steadies the world.

She is the upswell of iron seas
beneath the oily clouds,
movement and magic,
the reptile at the earth's root,
knowing, unspeaking.

To catch her thoughts
is to bathe in jade fire.

Fenris

Steaming tears and blood
carve runnels in the ice
of the black gulf.

Devastation lies chained;
six impossibilities binding
the All-Father's doom,
averting the day of fate
and shifting the path that leads
to the cold singularity
where all our realities—
all that is,
all that has been,
all that will be—
fold in upon themselves
and are swallowed up
by the wolf's merciless rage.

Baldur

His fire hidden
in a cloak, thick
and dark as a pall of smoke,
there is, now, no thought,
no calculation;
he is pure action
stepping from the night
into the shining hall.

He has no friends here
and no one greets him
as he moves smoothly
through the crowd
to stand beside his nephew.

Into the blind God's hand
he presses a twisted
black dart and whispers.

Throw it and see what happens.

Then he turns on his heel
and leaves.

Hodur speaks.

I neither hated my brother
nor envied him;
we complemented one another;
without my shadow
he was too bright to behold,

without his light
I was too dark to see.

Loki speaks.

I am not much given to regrets;
we do what we have to.

Baldur once said to me—
They have made of me
an object of amusement;
what was a symbol of greatness,
now diminishes me.

When it was done I fled the hall
and hid in the wilds;
they found me and,
in the form of a shimmering fish,
caught me in the net
of my own cleverness.

Before my eyes
they tore my son apart
and, with his guts,
bound me to a rock.

My wife stayed to tend me
and even my brother
would come sometimes
and sit silently beside me.

I don't know if it was sympathy
or whether he was afraid

that I too, in torment,
might drag some wisdom
from the void.

Hyrrokin speaks.

Some people have lived so long
they forget that nothing
lasts forever;
with Baldur fallen
they all felt Death's cold breath
upon their necks.

Robbed of certainty,
they lost their senses;
they mourned him so wildly
and poured up such treasures
about his corpse,
they could not release him
and called for help
from an older and darker power.

I came.

Old One-eye understood;
I saw him whispering
in the boy's dead ear,
before I dragged him off the strand
and set him to drift
upon the tides.

Then I rode home laughing!

My kin will not mourn for Baldur,

for he will rise again.

We would rather weep for the Gods
trapped in their blinkered
and unchanging present.

Baldur speaks.

My cousin is not unkind;
my brother, my wife and I
dine at her table,
and wander, at liberty,
across her wide lands.

She makes the ages brief
till that day comes
when we shall rise again
to the light.

Ship of Nails

At the last all paths
lead to the End.

There at Time's far shore
My Lady builds
a ship of nails.

Its hull is memory,
its timbers hold
the siren spiral songs
of our humanities.

Within, we cross
eternal seas
to a field of light
and shadow,
there to stand and war,
to bear our witness
against life unending.

If the harp is struck
and battle joined
we can only overcome.

For we are the Dead
and the Dead fear nothing.

The Dragon

A mother of serpents,
translucent as death,
she is hygiene and chaos;
abhorring stillness
she devours corpses
at the bleak sea's
slow edge.

A strange compassion
resides in her
reeking breath,
her eyes are soft,
unblinking;
she lowers her scaly head,
nods ... she is silence,
a seed of empathy
and comfort,
an unlikely ally
in the hostile land.

Helheim

At the close of day
a lady waits,
wide are her lands,
fine are her halls.

There a man might
catch his thoughts,
glowing like coals
in the embers
of her hearth.

There a man might
walk through autumn woods,
count each bronze leaf,
and never need to hasten.

Comfort she gives
to the sick at heart,
rest to the weary.

A child of iron and fire,
she knows what it is
to be lost.

Sister to the wolf
and the snake,
she knows the pain
of separation
and loves you for it.

So, if there you see her,
kiss her living hand for me

and say her realm is fairest.

Say, the horse
desires the bridle,
the falcon longs
for the arm of his Queen.

Tell her
that the cut rose
hungers for the soil.

The Cage

I dreamt a cage
of black iron,
and in the cage
I dreamt a crow,
and though he was me,
I could not free him.

Surt speaks.

Picture this,
the birth and death
of universes.

All matter,
all energy,
all that you are,
each cell and molecule,
every impulse and spark,
compressed within a point
of unutterable darkness,
and within that point
see a raging black fire.

That is me.

I am the inferno
that powers the explosion
that casts all life across
the Gap.

Now picture this.

A universe grown cold,
burned out stars
collapsing in upon themselves,
withdrawing to the centre,
to a single point
of unutterable darkness,
and within that point
see a raging black fire.

This is the place,
the boundary between times
which is no time,
where Odin hangs upon the Tree,
where Loki writhes
within his bonds,
this is the place of sacrifice
and the source of Power,
the birth and death
of all the worlds.

Can you accept
that one day you will not be,
and yet that you will be all,
flesh and stone,
fire, will and water,
each cell and molecule
every impulse and spark,
together with all matter
there compressed
inside the point
wherein I rage?

Can you accept
that once you were nothing,

and yet were the entirety of creation,
flesh and stone,
fire, will and water,
each cell and molecule
every impulse and spark,
together with all matter
there compressed
inside the point
wherein I raged?

Wide-spreading,
tall-standing,
in the wood I saw
trees like worlds.

I saw rivers and waterfalls
glisten on silver trunks,
I saw the webs of spiders
and the dreys of squirrels;
I saw the movement
of wind and sunlight.

I saw, in the distant meadow,
a crow skimming the high grass.

The Norns

In the narrow crook
of a twisted root
Grandmother Spider sits
spinning, shaping,
twisting ragged time;
her dreams
are warp and weft,
her memories
a warm birth
in the languid,
sacred land
where ice and fire
steamed existence
into being.

Mother weaves;
entranced by process
and potentialities,
she peers along
diminishing lines
of fate.

Daughter clambers
through the tangles,
tugs them apart,
slips through the gaps,
shears in hand;
she cuts and catches
the loose end,
ties off a knot,
moves on.

These women
require nothing,
fear nothing,
no one-eyed man,
no flame-haired wanderer,
no completions.

Endings are the currents
through which they swim.

Aurvandil's Journey

On a summer day
with the rising light
the Little Fathers rouse
the Wanderer from sleep
and sing him out of doors;
into his head
the Little Mothers sing
the purple distances,
say 'At this time of year
the Poison River
can be crossed
with a good staff
and a stout pair of boots!'

On the further bank
worlds unfurl before him;
he hears the Wayspirits' song
rise and fall on the gentle breeze,
senses their movements
deep in the sweet heather.

***

At Midgard's edge,
on a narrow bar
of sand and bitter grass,
he stands and fires arrows
into the skies.

The waters seethe
and swell
and the Sea Snake

surges from the depths
to loom above the sleeping shore.

Her voice is sand
ground between stones.

'Why, Wanderer,
do you shoot at the heavens?
Your arrows fall
and pierce the sea's skin,
marred with the blood of stars!'

He laughs and looses
another dart.

'I hunt the light
that I might be higher!'

***

On Lyngvi's Isle,
in the cave of ice,
he draws knife across palm;
watches thick blood
pool and steam.

The Wolf's question,
a grate of ice
rending the valley's
rocky walls.

'Why do you do this thing?'

He tips his hand.

'I mix my blood with yours
that I might understand!'

***

Beneath the moon,
drum in hand,
he sits at the foot
of the Volva's seat.

'What do you want to know?'
She whispers.

He sings.

'The future is a hollow egg,
I want to see inside!'

***

On a strand
of rocks and bones
he munches
slivers of flesh
sliced from the bodies
of the rotting dead.

'Why,' the Dragon asks,
'Do *you* eat corpses
on death's shore?'

'I devour death
as it devours me!'

Her yellow eyes
are lanterns in the gloom;
she lowers her head.

'Perhaps it is time
you went home.'

***

At the water's edge
he shivers as the Spirits rage.

'In winter the Poison River
freezes bones, ruins flesh!
Your staff is broken,
your boots are in shreds,
now you will surely die!'

'It is not yet time!'
He howls and shoots
at flurry and drift,
laughs as the Spirits scatter.

***

The Thunderer finds him
half buried in the snow.

'Wanderer!
In winter the Poison River
freezes bones, ruins flesh!
Your staff is broken,
your boots are in shreds.

Let me carry you
to the other side!'

Red-Beard laughs,
snaps a toe
from frozen foot;
casts it high.

'You will not need this,
and the Poison River
demands a toll!'

***

On the farther shore
the Worlds unfurl before them.

'What now, my friend?
Your feet are ruined;
you will not walk far.'

'I will now go home,
the Little Fathers sing me back,
the Little Mothers fill
my head with the scent
of good black earth.

If I cannot walk,
I will borrow a horse!'

***

Beneath blue skies
chill waters glint,

exuberant hoofbeats
shatter the brittle air.

He rides the gusts,
rides the road home,
sings the contours
of wind and hillside,
sings the low throated
shape of the land.

Part 2:

The Dis

:ᛟᚾᛖ·ᚱᛟᛟᛏ·ᚹᛁᛚᛚ·ᚾᛟᛏ·ᚠᛉᛞ:

:ᚨ·ᛏᚱᛉ·ᚠᛟᚱ·ᛚᛟᛝ:

:ᚾᛟᚱ·ᚹᛁᛚᛚ·ᛟᚾᛖ·ᚺᛇᚱ·ᛚᛟᚹᛖᚱ:

:ᚨ·ᛞᚨᚱᛏᛖᚾᛋ·ᛒᚨᛚ:

:ᚨᚾᛞᛚ·ᛉᛈ·ᚦᛖ·ᛚᚨᛏᛞ·ᚨᛏ·ᛒᛇ:

The Dis

With the exception of 'Ull' which came as a kind of introduction, these poems are the reminiscences of a Dís, or female ancestral Spirit. Despite my efforts to 'bind her Telling in time and place' (see 'Educated Guesses' in the notes) the Dís' words are best left to speak for themselves. For my part, I have peered into the Sokkvabek and this is what I have seen.

You would give
my words more weight,
speak my nature,
sing my origin,
you would bind
the Telling
in time and place.

What can I say?

There was a river,
shallow with rocky banks;
a wooded mountain
upon whose peak
tufts of ragged cloud
would sometimes cling.

In summer
the sun barely set,
in winter
it barely rose.

Once I travelled,
a hard weeks journey,
and saw the wide sea
dully glint beneath the mist.

Ull

He is all the colours of the yew;
eyes of darkest green,
skin weathered bark
bronzed by the first touch
of the rising sun.

A sweep of his arm
enwraps the dormant land,
at rest beneath
its coverlet of snow.

He speaks.

Your people hunted here,
followed the deer,
gathered berries
and built their camps
in amongst the spruce.

You believe your heart
is torn ... it is not so.

Your many hearts
are all entire.

One root will not feed
a tree for long,
nor will one hair cover
a marten's back
and keep the cold at bay.

Corners

I can tell the stories,
recite your lore
but it is not mine.

Mine is a world of corners,
above, below, besides,
born from a green egg.

A thing of fire
laughs in my head
at a chalk-faced death
it doesn't fear.

My Spirits
are stream and forest,
wind and snow,
the quiet reindeer
and the clever marten
chattering in the pines.

Connections

How do I come to you?

Down the Stream
I slither, a silver fish
bright with thought,
slick with memory.

I am here...
and where I was,
in all those places in between.

I have seen such things,
and yet remain
the old woman
riding the reindeer,
the young girl,
alone amidst the spruce,
mumbling to the little Gods.

Arrival

When first we came
to the place
that became my home,
we had to cross
a shallow river.

On the far side
 was a bank of shingle.

Here my father
raised some poles
for the Spirits
smeared with soot
and white ash.

It was a good place,
rich with berries
and mushrooms;
there were no people
but plenty of food for the deer.

Gratitude

My father would grumble
that we didn't have
a proper hunting god.

However, he would hang
a piece of every catch
on this tree or that
for the forest Gods;
we usually had enough.

Life

I was still young, a girl,
when the Old Woman
called me to her tent
and bound strips of marten fur
about my hands.

I thought I would be a great witch
and do remarkable things!

Mostly I treated the reindeer,
sang over our sick;
sometimes I cured them,
sometimes they died;
I learned to read the signs.

My father and, later,
my brother sent me
to the woods to talk
with the Spirits.

With everyone else
I shivered in winter,
sweated in summer.

Mask

The Old Woman before me
was my father's aunt;
she had a wooden mask
with little horns,
whitened with ash and chalk.

She would wear it
when the White One
moved within her.

It came to me
when she died
but I rarely used it.

In the end I fastened it
to an old tree.

Gods

The White One
is a board of wood,
gouged out eyes and mouth.

She is whitened with ash
and chalk, this face
of death fringed
with long black hair,
topped with tiny horns
carved from the antlers
of a female deer.

The Other has no face.

It is a ball of fire,
sometimes ablaze,
sometimes quiet embers
in my head.

It smirks, laughs,
cajoles and insults;
it peers out from my eyes
and tells me what it sees.

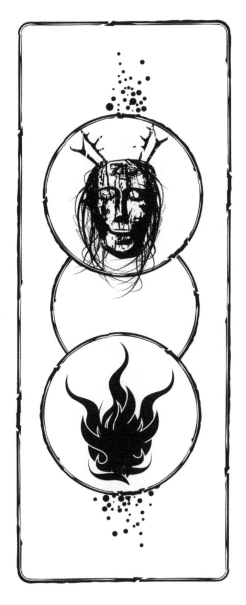

Possession

The Other used to move
in my head
like fire through the forest.

It was a ball of hot light
heaving me,
this way and that.

It would push past,
peer through my eyes
stripping sight and reality
back to bare nature.

It could be rough
but was not unkind;
when it rode me
I nestled
in the backmost corner
of my skull
and watched
through a veil of cobwebs.

The Marten

The Marten, he's a fine fellow!

I wear his hide
wrapped about my hands and wrists.
He's sharp and willing,
quick fire dancing
along the crusted bough,
a flash of yellow
ablaze in the shadows
of the forest.

On the grey rocks
he is a hunter,
a creature of speed
and cunning.

Look through his eyes!

He sees other worlds
and, if you listen
and understand,
he has tales to tell
of bitter winters
and joyous summers,
the triumph of the catch,
the savour of blood,
warm in his throat.

Departure

My grandson was a strong man
with yellow hair and blue eyes
like my father.

He was kind
and good with the deer.

When I grew too old to walk far
he gave me a white buck
to ride on.

When I died
it had just begun to snow.

Death

This is how it happened.

There was no wind
and the snow gently fell.
Unable to move,
I watched the grey sky,
felt the cold earth
beneath my back,
heard the Spirits
chitter their uncertainty.

Her coming was soft and sudden.
She stood above me,
more beautiful
than I expected,
less frightening
than the Old Woman's mask.

She knelt and her hair
fell about her shoulders;
I saw that at the end
of each black strand
was a finger's width
of purest white.

She removed my hand
from its mitten,
held it, simply said—
'Daughter.....'

That is it;
I can say no more.

ᛌ ᚱ ᚢ ᛁ ᛏ ᚠ ᛗ ᛋ ᛊ ᛁ ᛋ ᚾ ᚠ ᛈ ᛗ ᚱ ᛁ ᛋ ᛁ ᛈ
ᛏ ᛗ ᛁ ᚦ ᚱ ᚾ ᛊ ᛁ ᛈ ᛈ ᚠ ᚠ ᛁ ᛟ
ᚾ ᚠ ᛈ ᛗ ᚱ ᛋ ᛚ ᛗ ᚨ ᚠ ᛚ ᚱ ᚨ ᛋ ᛈ ᛗ ᛋ ᛈ
ᚦ ᚠ ᛏ ᛗ ᚱ ᚦ ᛈ ᛈ ᛋ ᚠ ᛁ ᚨ ᚠ ᚱ ᛉ ᚦ ᛗ ᛋ
ᚦ ᚠ ᛈ ᛋ ᚠ ᛉ ᛋ ᛈ
ᚦ ᚠ ᛈ ᛋ ᛒ ᛉ ᛏ ᚱ ᚦ ᛗ ᚨ ᚱ ᚦ ᛗ ᚱ ᛋ
ᚠ ᚱ ᛈ ᚾ ᚠ ᛏ ᚦ ᛋ ᛈ ᚾ ᚠ ᛈ ᛗ ᚨ ᚱ ᛁ ᛗ
ᚦ ᚠ ᛈ ᛋ ᛒ ᛉ ᛏ ᚱ ᚦ ᛗ ᚨ ᚱ ᚦ ᛗ ᚱ ᛋ
ᚠ ᚱ ᛏ ᛏ ᚦ ᛈ ᚦ ᚦ ᛋ ᛈ ᚠ ᚱ ᛗ

An Afterword: How The Other Made The World

A young woman kneels on a shingle beach by a blue lake fringed with forest.

Her black hair is pulled back at her crown in a long ponytail, her skin is tanned, her eyes grey. About her hands and wrists are bound ragged strips of reddish hide. Before her sit five children of various sizes: three boys—one fair, one dark, one redhead; two girls—one fair, one dark. They are twisting large handfuls of grass into thick bundles in order to make conical hats like the one the blond boy is already wearing. While they work they sing. After a short while the song finishes and they chatter until the woman raises her hand for silence and begins to speak...

At first this Middle World
was just air above
and sea beneath;
all that lived here were fishes
and swimming birds.

It was always night
and the many nations
of ducks would gather
to bob on the calm water,
look up at the heavens
and wonder,
'What is it like to be a star?'

One time the Other
was riding past
on a restless breeze;
it looked down and saw them,
wondered,
'What is it like to be a duck?'

Down it swooped,
plucked an errant plume
from a quiet wavetop,
breathed on it,
sang the words of power;
one became two,
two became four,
four became six
and soon the Other
had enough to weave
a dappled cloak
of gold and brown,
shimmering feathers.

Around its shoulders
it drew the cloak
and, so, became a duck.

The Other was not shy;
down it—or she
as we must now call her—
swooped to bob
with the other ducks,
to gossip about the weather
and the taste of water,
to admire the menfolk
with their glistening heads
of greeny black.

The Other was not shy;
shamelessly she flirted
with the handsome drakes
until she felt new life
surge within her.

'Now,' she thought,
'I will need somewhere
to bring it forth!'

She called to her side
the many nations
of the ducks, said—
'Dive down into the
inky waters,
fetch from the Ocean's floor
weeds and mud
that I might make
a nest in which
to lay my egg!'

And down the ducks plunged,
down until their eyes bulged,
until they thought
their lungs would burst;
but no Ocean floor
could they find,
no weed and mud
for the making
of the Other's nest.

And so the Other
called to her side
all the many nations
of the diving birds, said—
'Dive down into the
inky waters,
fetch from the Ocean's floor
weeds and mud

that I might make
a nest in which
to lay my egg!'

And down they plunged,
divers and grebes and mergansers,
down into the inky depths,
down to the Ocean floor to pluck
sturdy fronds of weed,
down to the Ocean floor to scoop
beak and billfulls of slippery mud.

The Other was not slow;
quick as thought
she wove the sturdy fronds,
lined them with the slippery mud,
made a nest to float,
tight as a drum
on the gentle waters.

And now the Other
sat within it,
laid a single egg,
glossy and smooth,
green as a late summer leaf.

The time of ducks
is not the same as that of men
so who can say how long
the Other sat and warmed her egg?

Still, soon enough,
she felt it hatch.

First to emerge were
the glowing sun
and the shining moon;
next the mothers
and fathers of
the thousand clouds
bubbled forth
and raced away
to the sky's four corners.

The Other looked and saw
the perfect blue
of the heavens,
saw the sun and moonlight glisten
on the wavelets,
saw that it was good,
but not quite good enough!

She took the broken shell,
green as a late summer leaf,
sang it, shaped it, made
the wide-spreading earth,
clothed with trees and grasses,
adorned with flowers
of every colour.

And in the young forests
she formed the many nations
of the land,
bear and beetle,
wolf and marten,
the roaming reindeer,
the two-footed man
that follows in her tracks.

Then the Other
clacked her beak with pleasure,
slipped from her back
the cloak of feathers,
again became a spirit,
rose upon the breeze and said—
'Who would have thought
that being a duck
was so much fun?'

Mythological Notes

UPG, PCPG, Etc.

Personal gnosis is a term used to refer to spiritual insights and revelations gained through any one of a number of magico-religious practices ranging from direct divine revelation to ordeal and trancework. Sometimes it is possible for one person's insight to be confirmed by another person or persons who have had a similar or at least corroborative experience. This is referred to as Peer Corroborated Personal Gnosis (PCPG). Often, however, it is not possible to confirm matters in this way, even if there is no reason at all to doubt the insight. Here we speak of Unverified Personal Gnosis (UPG).

The Three Races

There are a number of races living in the Nine Worlds, but the three most relevant to this work are the Jötnar, the Vanir and the Aesir. The Jötnar are usually referred to as 'Giants' in English, but I prefer to avoid this term as it has implications of size which are not always applicable. The Jötnar, in their natures, mirror the wilder primal energies of the natural world, and their Gods—the Rökkr—are much concerned with hunting, with the wilderness, and consequently with death, decay and regeneration. The Vanir, the people of Vili, are more concerned with agriculture and with the fertility of the earth and all living things. The Aesir are the Gods of the Norse aristocracy, representing both martial and artistic virtues. They are more conservative than the other two races, being much concerned with social and divine order and its maintenance. These characterisations are, of course, only very general as the functions of each pantheon and, indeed, of individual deities tend to overlap a great deal. The Aesir and the Jötnar remain generally hostile to one another despite much fraternisation and intermarriage, while the Vanir are broadly allied to the Aesir but considerably less hostile towards the Jötnar.

Skald

Skalds were the poets and singers of the ancient Norse world. They were often travellers wandering from hall to hall performing poems and songs and telling stories often to the accompaniment of harp or other musical instrument.

Magpie Woman

Magpie Woman is Hela, Queen of Helheim, the Underworld and Realm of the Dead. Skadhi is the Goddess of Skiing, hunting and therefore of death. More precisely she is the Deity that presides over the instant when life ceases whereas Hela oversees the whole process of death, afterlife and rebirth.

Hengistbury Head

Modron is the Autumn Equinox. Hengistbury Head is a sandstone headland that guards the approach to Christchurch harbour and protrudes out into the English Channel. There is evidence of human habitation here that stretches back to times when the Channel was still a grassy plain where wild horses roamed.

Mordgud

Mordgud is a warrior maiden, possibly a sister to Hela and daughter of Loki, who guards the Bridge of Knives that spans the chasm before the walls of Helheim. The blades of which the walkway is made will not cut the feet of those who do not fear. Mordgud acts as a guardian of the Dead and also as a psychopomp, guiding them safely into her sister's realm. Her role also includes keeping out the living!

Truth

They say that Loki is the Prince of Lies. Actually, he tells the truth, which is far worse!

Surt

The oldest and most powerful of all beings, Surt begins the process of creation when he moves his world of fire (Muspelheim) closer to Niflheim and starts the thaw that leads to the birth of Aurgelmir and, indirectly, to the making of the Nine Worlds. It is prophesied that he will survive Ragnarök (the end of the worlds) and together with his sons will scour clean creation thus enabling a new universe to arise. This process may have occurred before on countless occasions. Grandmother is Urd, the oldest of the three Norns who sit at the foot of the World-Tree weaving the fates of all creatures; One-Eye is Odin; Red-Beard is Thor, strongest of the Gods; World-Walker is Loki.

Ask and Embla

Ask and Embla were the first man and woman, created and animated by Odin and his brothers from two uprooted trees they found while walking by the seashore one day. Ask was made from the trunk of an ash tree and Embla from an elm. After their creation they seem to have been somewhat neglected and had to be rescued from the cataclysmic flood that followed the killing of Aurgelmir by the Frost-Giant Bergelmir.

The Three Brothers

Aurgelmir, known as Ymir to the Aesir, was the great primal frost giant from whose body the Nine Worlds were made. He was murdered and dismembered by the ancient trinity of the Norse tradition—Odin, Vili and Ve.

AllFather

The All-Father is Odin, father of Gods and men, King of Asgard and brother, or blood-brother to Loki (the exact nature of their relationship is unclear and Loki likes to give contradictory accounts). Odin's primary occupation is the pursuit of wisdom. He sacrificed himself on the World-Tree to obtain the mysteries of the Runes, gave up his eye to see the future. His overriding purpose is now to avert the very fate he saw—Ragnarök, the Day of Doom.

Frigga

Frigga is the wife of Odin, mother of Baldur and Queen of Asgard. Vili's people are the Vanir, the Gods of Fertility and the Land. They also have a strong connection with the sea as their King is Njord (Hoenir/Vili) the God of Ships and Sea-Farers.

The Old Queen And The New

The original Queen of the Underworld (then known as Jormundgrund) was the first Hel. During her reign the realm was a dreary and forbidding place. For some reason, never fully explained, she either died or simply went away, closing the great iron gates behind her abandoning her charges and clearing the way for Hela to assume her rightful place.

The Iron Wood

Situated in Jötunheim (the world of the Giants) Jarnvidr, the Iron Wood, is the source of all the magic in the Nine Worlds. It is the realm of Angrboda, wife of Loki, and the birthplace of her children Hela, Fenris and Jormungand.

Angrboda

Angrboda, the Witch-Queen of the Iron Wood, was burned three times by the Aesir but through her own magic she rose twice. After the third occasion, Loki rescued her charred heart, placed it in his mouth and carried it home to the Iron Wood where he was able to revive her again.

Loki

The God of Fire and Trickster of the Northern Tradition, Loki is the bête noir of Odin and the Aesir. He is the father of Hela and with her is the most prominent of the Rökkr.

World Serpent

While still young Jormungand, the half fish half snake daughter of Angrboda and Loki was kidnapped by the Gods. She escaped and fell into the ocean that surrounds Middle-Earth and there she swims still, a force of chaos whose endless movement prevents stagnation.

Fenris

The spirit of destruction, Fenris was kidnapped and then bound by the Gods. He lies chained awaiting Ragnarök, planning his revenge on all creation. It is prophesied that he will kill and devour Odin himself on the last day before Vidar, Odin's son, then kills him.

Baldur

The story of Baldur is one of the best known of all Norse myths. His mother, Frigga, obtains oaths from all the rocks and metals, animals and plants that they will not harm him. His immunity means that the Gods entertain themselves by throwing weapons at him and lacing his meals with deadly poisons. It so happens, however, that Frigga has not got round to the apparently harmless mistletoe. Loki, who is seeking revenge for the chaining of his own son Fenris, discovers this and makes an enchanted dart from the little plant. He tricks Baldur's brother Hodur into throwing this and Baldur is killed. The Gods try to redeem the God of Light from Helheim but cannot do so. They do, however, take their own revenge on Loki by binding him to a rock with the entrails of another of his sons, Narvi. Baldur remains in Helheim but it is prophesied that he will rise again after Ragnarök to take Odin's place as King of the Gods.

Ship of Nails

Surt and Hela collect the toe and finger nails of the Dead and from them are building a great ship—Naglfari. Its completion will mark the end of the world, Ragnarök, and then the hosts of the Dead will climb on board and sail out to fight a final great battle with the Gods.

The Dragon

Nidhogg dwells on the borders of Niflheim (the world of ice and snow) and Helheim. There she devours corpses and nibbles at the roots of the World-Tree, causing it to put out new growth and thereby to remain strong.

Helheim

Hela, having taken up her Queenship of the Underworld, reshaped it and created a place of rest and regeneration for all the Dead not swept up into Valhalla or the abodes of the various other Gods.

The Cage

For Surt see note above. Odin hung on the World-Tree for nine days and nights to gain wisdom, Loki went through his own ordeal bound to a rock in the bowels of the earth.

The Norns

The three fates who sit at the foot of the World Tree. Urd, the spinner—what has been; Verdandhi, the weaver—that which is becoming; and Skuld, who cuts the thread—what should be.

Aurvandil's Journey

An enigmatic figure in Germanic mythology, Aurvandil (also known as Egil) was clearly once important, although little is known about him now. He was the first husband of Sif, the Corn Goddess who later married Thor. He subsequently married Groa, an important Jötun witch and healer. With the latter he is the father of Svipdag, Thjalfi and Roskva, all significant figures in Norse mythology. He pops up in some unexpected places in later folklore as Earendel, 'the brightest Angel over Middle-Earth' in the Christian Anglo-Saxon poem of the same name; as the father of Amleth, Prince of Denmark and the prototype of Shakespeare's Hamlet; and also as Earendil the Mariner in Tolkien's 'Lord of the Rings'. He is always closely linked with stars and in the one specific myth that tells of him he is carried across a freezing landscape by his friend and travelling companion, the God Thor (Red-Beard) who snaps off one of Aurvandil's frozen toes. The Thunder God flings the toe into the night sky where it becomes a star, possibly Venus, Rigel or Alcor.

The Dís: Some Educated Guesses

We are here in the realm not so much of unverified as unverifiable personal gnosis. My guesses are as follows:

With regards to location, the Dís says that the sun barely sets in summer and barely rises in winter. This places her just south of the Arctic Circle. My original theory was that she was therefore either in Scandinavia, Karelia or North-western Russia. This still seems most likely but I am aware that, today, in order to find reindeer large enough to ride you have to go much further east into Siberia. I could, of course be completely wrong, as there is some archaeological evidence of reindeer herding in the post-glacial period at least as far south as my home in southern England.

As regards time, the Dís never mentions metal and therefore probably lived before the introduction of Iron into the Far North of Europe. This means before the Germanic, and earlier Celtic, incursions into Scandinavia. Her mythology is not Norse or even recognisably Indo-European. The White One and the Other seem similar in nature to Hela and Loki but not explicitly so. Her origin myth has some features that would seem to be Finnic—creation of the world from a bird's egg for example.

By the way, the Sokkvabek is the River of Time that flows through Asgard and is watched over by the goddess Saga. Looking into its depths it is possible, but not easy, to see all that has been, all that is and all that might be.

Ull

A God of Hunting and skiing, Ull is in some ways a male counterpart to the Goddess Skadhi. He was much respected by the Aesir and, when Odin was temporarily ousted as their ruler, Ull was chosen to replace him and thus ruled for a time as King of the Gods. After a while Odin returned and Ull breathed a sigh of relief and returned to his beloved mountains and forests. Ull is closely linked with Yew trees in general and the World-Tree (which is a yew in some of the older accounts) in specific.

The Marten

The Pine Marten is a member of the weasel family found in both coniferous forests and rocky areas across Northern Europe. It preys mostly on small mammals, birds, insects, frogs, and carrion. They are dark red-brown in colour with a yellowish 'bib' on their chest. Adults are about the size of a domestic cat.

Further Reading

Should anyone wish to learn more about the Northern Tradition, and the Rökkr and Jötnar in particular, I strongly recommend Raven Kaldera's Northern Tradition Shamanism series of books, published by the Asphodel Press, which provide a wealth of lore and anecdotal accounts of the Giants of the Northern Tradition and their Gods. For the Aesir's perspective try Kevin Crossley-Holland's *The Norse Myths* (Pantheon Press) and, of course, the Icelandic Eddas and the various other Scandinavian sagas.

About the Author

When away from his day job as a postman, Andrew Gyll is a poet and storyteller with a keen interest in the mythology and folklore of Northern Europe. He lives in Dorset, Southern England.

Photo by Lizard Woman